7966

A New True Book

THE DECLARATION OF INDEPENDENCE

By Dennis B. Fradin

CHILDRENS PRESS ®

CHICAGO

PHOTO CREDITS

©Cameramann International, Ltd.—4 (bottom right)

Historical Pictures Service, Chicago—Cover, 2, 6, 7, 10, 11, 13 (2 photos), 14 (2 photos), 17, 20, 21, 23 (2 photos), 25, 30, 33, 35, 37

Journalism Services: ©Joseph Jacobson—4 (top)
©Harvey Moshman—4 (bottom left)

Library of Congress—15, 18, 27

North Wind Picture Archives—9, 29, 39, 41, 42

Third Coast Stock Source:
©William Meyer—45 (2 photos)

Cover: The signing of The Declaration of Independence

The Spirit of '76 honors the patriots who fought in the American Revolution.

For David Polster

Library of Congress Cataloging-in-Publication Data

Fradin, Dennis B.
    The Declaration of Independence.

    (A New true book)
    Includes index.
    Summary: Examines the political situation in America at the time of the troubles between England and her colonies there and describes how the Declaration of Independence was written and accepted.
    1. United States. Declaration of Independence—Juvenile literature. 2. United States—Politics and government—Revolution, 1775-1783—Juvenile literature.
[1. United States. Declaration of Independence.
2. United States—Politics and government—Revolution, 1775-1783] I. Title
E221.F8   1988   973.3'13   88-11870
ISBN 0-516-01153-7

TABLE OF CONTENTS

Fireworks and parades are part of every Fourth of July celebration.

WHAT IS THE DECLARATION OF INDEPENDENCE?

Every Fourth of July, people in the United States enjoy a holiday. Stores and schools close. People go to parades and fireworks shows.

July Fourth is a holiday because of what happened on July 4, 1776. On that day, American lawmakers approved the Declaration of Independence.

The Declaration of Independence is read in Philadelphia in 1776.

The Declaration said that the thirteen American colonies, which had long been ruled by England, were now free. It declared that a new country had been formed—the United States of America.

THE YEARS BEFORE THE TROUBLES WITH ENGLAND

In 1607 England built its first permanent town in America at Jamestown, Virginia. By the early 1700s, England ruled thirteen colonies in America. The thirteen were Virginia,

The Virginia Colony began in 1607.

Massachusetts, New Hampshire, New York, Connecticut, Maryland, Rhode Island, Delaware, Pennsylvania, North Carolina, New Jersey, South Carolina, and Georgia.

The Swedish settlers were the first to build log cabins in America.

England's kings and queens sent Englishmen to govern the Thirteen Colonies. Most of the colonists also came from England. Other colonists came from Germany, Scotland, Ireland, The Netherlands, Sweden, and France.

The Pilgrims came to America for religious reasons.

People made the long, dangerous voyage across the Atlantic Ocean to America for many reasons. Many sought a place where they could worship freely. Others wanted land. Some sought treasure or adventure.

The Indians taught the Pilgrims how to plant corn.
It became their most important food crop.

In America, the colonists cut down trees and built farms, churches, and schools. They planted corn and other crops. English rulers usually gave the colonists plenty of freedom. The colonists had few complaints until the 1760s.

THE TROUBLES
WITH ENGLAND BEGIN

Trouble began when the
English rulers started
taxing colonists. England
needed to pay for a war it
had won against France in
1763. English lawmakers
decided to raise the money
by taxing the colonists.
They tried to make the
Americans pay taxes on
items such as sugar, tea,
paper, paint, and newspapers.
Because they had not

Angry citizens of Boston read about the Stamp Tax (left). In a later protest, patriots, dressed up as Indians, dumped a shipment of taxed tea into Boston Harbor (above).

taken part in making the tax laws, the colonists did not want to pay these taxes. They held protest meetings. They rioted. To protest England's tax on tea, Americans dumped the tea into Boston Harbor in 1773. This was called the *Boston Tea Party.*

13

England sent soldiers to keep order. The colonists hated being watched by these "redcoats." English rulers also angered the colonists by telling them to provide housing and supplies for the soldiers.

England forced Americans (left) to work for the British navy. English soldiers in Boston (below) often fought the American patriots.

George Washington,
Thomas Jefferson,
and Alexander
Hamilton were
members of the First
Continental Congress.

In 1774 the Americans held a big meeting in Philadelphia. They discussed how to handle their problems with England. This meeting was called the *First Continental Congress*

and lasted about two months.
Every colony except Georgia
sent delegates to the First
Continental Congress.

Very few of the fifty-six
delegates wanted
independence from
England. But they all
wanted fairer treatment
from England. Congress
sent messages to
England's King George III
asking for justice. They

The American government sent representatives to England to plead for justice from the king's council.

planned to meet in spring of 1775 if England did not make changes.

King George III would not accept the Americans' demands. In fact, fighting between the colonists and the redcoats began. The

The Battle of Lexington marked the beginning
of the shooting war between England and America.

first battles were fought
at Lexington and Concord,
Massachusetts, in April of
1775. The next month the
Second Continental Congress
opened in Philadelphia.

CONGRESS ASKS FOR A DECLARATION OF INDEPENDENCE

Despite the outbreak of war, few delegates to the Second Continental Congress favored American independence. Many thought that, after a little more fighting, England would make up with America.

But between spring of 1775 and summer of 1776 more Americans decided

View of The ATTACK on BUNKER's HILL, with the Burning of CHARLES TOWN, June 17.1775.

in favor of independence.
There were several reasons
why. On June 17, 1775 the
English won the bloody
Battle of Bunker Hill, near
Boston. About 1,000 English
and 400 American soldiers
were killed or wounded.
After Bunker Hill, neither
side was in a mood to
make up.

German soldiers, called Hessians, were hired by England to fight the Americans.

The colonists also learned that the king had hired thousands of German soldiers, called *Hessians*, to fight against them. Americans were bitter about this and turned against English rule even more.

Common Sense, a book published in January of 1776, helped convince Americans to form a new country. It was written by Thomas Paine, an Englishman who had come to live in Philadelphia in 1774. *Common Sense* explained why America should be independent. Paine wrote that rule by kings and queens deprived people of their rights. He also wrote that it was silly

COMMON SENSE;

ADDRESSED TO THE

INHABITANTS

OF

AMERICA,

On the following interesting

SUBJECTS.

I. Of the Origin and Design of Government in general, with concise Remarks on the English Constitution.

II. Of Monarchy and Hereditary Succession.

III. Thoughts on the present State of American Affairs.

IV. Of the present Ability of America, with some miscellaneous Reflections.

Man knows no Master save creating HEAVEN,
Or those whom choice and common good ordain.
THOMSON.

PHILADELPHIA:
Printed, and Sold, by R. BELL, in Third-Street.
MDCCLXXVI.

Thomas Paine (above) was the author of *Common Sense* (right).

for an island (England) to rule a continent (North America). Thousands of Americans read *Common Sense* and agreed with its ideas.

By summer of 1776 a large number of Americans favored independence. But about as many people still opposed it. Some of those opposed were wealthy people who did business with England. They feared losing money if America broke away from England. Others thought that America was not yet ready to stand on its own.

The Second Continental Congress discussed

The Second Continental Congress met on May 10, 1775.

independence in spring of 1776. Among those for independence were John and Samuel Adams of Massachusetts, Benjamin Franklin of Pennsylvania, and Richard Henry Lee of Virginia. Those against independence included

John Dickinson of
Pennsylvania and Edward
Rutledge of South Carolina.

Finally, Congress
decided to vote on the
question in early July. But
what if the delegates voted
for independence? Congress
would need to explain why
America was breaking away
from England. Congress asked
a committee of five men to
write this explanation, or
Declaration of Independence.

WRITING THE DECLARATION OF INDEPENDENCE

The five men on the committee were John Adams of Massachusetts, Benjamin Franklin of Pennsylvania,

From left to right: Thomas Jefferson, Roger Sherman, Benjamin Franklin, Robert R. Livingston, John Adams

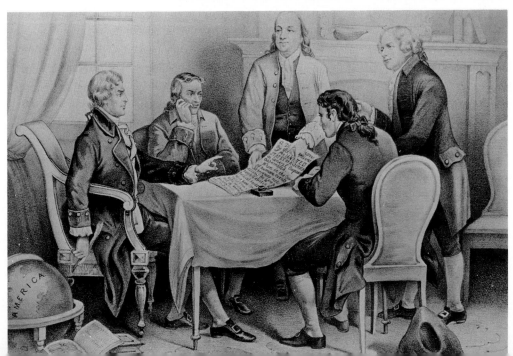

Robert R. Livingston of
New York, Roger Sherman
of Connecticut, and Thomas
Jefferson of Virginia.

Franklin was the most
famous man in Congress
and a good writer. But
the seventy-year-old
Franklin was sick, so he
couldn't write the Declaration.
Instead, thirty-three-year-old
Thomas Jefferson of
Virginia was chosen.

Jefferson worked on the
Declaration of Independence

Thomas Jefferson wrote and rewrote the Declaration of Independence.

during two weeks of late June 1776. He wrote it at his desk in his Philadelphia apartment at Market and Seventh streets. Jefferson showed his work to Ben

A few more changes were made to Jefferson's document by Benjamin Franklin and John Adams.

Franklin and John Adams, who made a few changes in it. The young Virginian then turned the paper in to Congress.

CONGRESS VOTES ON INDEPENDENCE

If Congress voted against independence, the Declaration would not be needed. The official vote was set for July 2, 1776. On Monday, July 1, 1776 Congress took a trial vote. Nine colonies favored independence. Pennsylvania and South Carolina were opposed. New York had told its delegates not to vote on the issue. One of Delaware's delegates wanted independence, one was opposed, and one had not reached Philadelphia yet.

The delegates knew that it wasn't good enough for *most* of the colonies to want independence. *All* of them had to want it, or the colonists might end up fighting each other. Before the big vote, the delegates

Painting shows the delegates at prayer.

for independence spoke to
those opposed or unsure.
The historic vote was then
held on Tuesday, July 2,
1776.

The nine colonies that
had favored independence
on July 1 held firm. South
Carolina voted "Yes" to go

along with the majority.
Pennsylvania chose
independence by a 3-2
vote when two delegates
who were opposed did not
vote. After an 80-mile ride
on horseback, Caesar Rodney
arrived in the nick of time
to swing Delaware's vote to
independence. New York
did not vote on July 2, but
made the vote unanimous
by approving independence
a few days later.

Delegates worked late into the night
trying to get representatives from all the
states to support independence from England.

Many delegates thought
that July 2—the day they
had voted for independence—
would be remembered as
the country's birthday.
Congress then studied
Thomas Jefferson's
Declaration.

APPROVING THE DECLARATION

Congress studied and discussed the Declaration of Independence on July 2, 3, and 4, 1776. The delegates made a few changes in Jefferson's paper. One big change that was approved took out a section condemning slavery. Several Southern states, where there were many slaves, insisted that this section be removed.

Delegates sign the
Declaration of
Independence.

On July 4, 1776,
Congress approved the
Declaration. The news was
sent across the new country.
People cheered as the
Declaration was read to
them. They shot off cannons
and burned English flags.

The top of the Declaration said IN CONGRESS, JULY 4, 1776. That was the date when Congress had approved the Declaration. People began celebrating that day as the nation's birthday instead of July 2. After two centuries, we still honor the day the Declaration was approved rather than the day Congress voted for independence.

Fifty-six Congressmen representing all thirteen states signed the

Handwritten facsimile signatures of the fifty-six delegates to the Declaration of Independence, including John Penn, Wm Floyd, John Hancock, John Hart, Wm Paca, Geo Read, Wm Hooper, Saml Adams, Geo Clymer, Step. Hopkins, Thos Nelson jr, Charles Carroll of Carrollton, Elbridge Gerry, Tho M:Kean, Roger Sherman, Saml Huntington, Wm Whipple, Thomas Lynch Junr, Geo Taylor, Josiah Bartlett, Benja Franklin, Wm Williams, Richd Stockton, John Morton, Oliver Wolcott, Jno Witherspoon, Geo Ross, Tho Stone, Samuel Chase, Robt Treat Paine, George Wythe, Matthew Thornton, Frans Lewis, Th Jefferson, Benja Harrison, Lewis Morris, Abra Clark, Phil Livingston, Casar Rodney, Arthur Middleton, Fras Hopkinson, Geo Walton, Carter Braxton, James Wilson, Richard Henry Lee, Thos Heyward Junr, Benjamin Rush, John Adams, Robt Morris, Lyman Hall, Joseph Hewes, Button Gwinnett, Francis Lightfoot Lee, William Ellery, Edward Rutledge, Jas Smith.

Department of State 1st April 1818. I Certify that this is a CORRECT Copy of the original Declaration of Independence deposited at this Department, and that I have compared all the signatures with those of the original and have found them EXACT IMITATIONS. John Quincy Adams

Copies of the signatures of the fifty-six delegates

Declaration. As President of the Second Continental Congress, John Hancock of Massachusetts signed first. Most of the delegates signed the Declaration in early August of 1776.

WHAT THE DECLARATION SAID

The Declaration said why Americans wanted freedom from England. It stated that all people "are created equal," and have the rights to "Life, Liberty and the pursuit of Happiness." The Declaration related nearly thirty ways that the English king was depriving Americans of those rights.

IN CONGRESS, JULY 4, 1776

The unanimous Declaration of the thirteen united States of America,

When in the Course of human events, it becomes necessary for one people to dissolve the political bands which have connected them with another, and to assume among the powers of the earth, the separate and equal station to which the Laws of Nature and of Nature's God entitle them, a decent respect to the opinions of mankind requires that they should declare the causes which impel them to the separation.

We hold these truths to be self-evident, that all men are created equal, that they are endowed by their Creator with certain unalienable Rights, that among these are Life, Liberty and the pursuit of Happiness. — That to secure these rights, Governments are instituted among Men, deriving their just powers from the consent of the governed, — That whenever any Form of Government becomes destructive of these ends, it is the Right of the People to alter or to abolish it, and to institute new Government, laying its foundation on such principles and organizing its powers in such form, as to them shall seem most likely to effect their Safety and Happiness. Prudence, indeed, will dictate that Governments long established should not be changed for light and transient causes; and accordingly all experience hath shewn, that mankind are more disposed to suffer, while evils are sufferable, than to right themselves by abolishing the forms to which they are accustomed. But when a long train of abuses and usurpations, pursuing invariably the same Object evinces a design to reduce them under absolute Despotism, it is their right, it is their duty, to throw off such Government, and to provide new Guards for their future security. — Such has been the patient sufferance of these Colonies; and such is now the necessity which constrains them to alter their former Systems of Government. The history of the present King of Great Britain is a history of repeated injuries and usurpations, all having in direct object the establishment of an absolute Tyranny over these States. To prove this, let Facts be submitted to a candid world.

He has refused his Assent to Laws, the most wholesome and necessary for the public good.

He has forbidden his Governors to pass Laws of immediate and pressing importance, unless suspended in their operation till his Assent should be obtained; and when so suspended, he has utterly neglected to attend to them.

He has refused to pass other Laws for the accommodation of large districts of people, unless those people would relinquish the right of Representation in the Legislature, a right inestimable to them and formidable to tyrants only.

He has called together legislative bodies at places unusual, uncomfortable, and distant from the depository of their public Records, for the sole purpose of fatiguing them into compliance with his measures.

He has dissolved Representative Houses repeatedly, for opposing with manly firmness his invasions on the rights of the people.

He has refused for a long time, after such dissolutions, to cause others to be elected; whereby the Legislative powers, incapable of Annihilation, have returned to the People at large for their exercise; the State remaining in the mean time exposed to all the dangers of invasion from without, and convulsions within.

He has endeavoured to prevent the population of these States; for that purpose obstructing the Laws for Naturalization of Foreigners; refusing to pass others to encourage their migrations hither, and raising the conditions of new Appropriations of Lands.

He has obstructed the Administration of Justice, by refusing his Assent to Laws for establishing Judiciary powers.

He has made Judges dependent on his Will alone, for the tenure of their offices, and the amount and payment of their salaries.

He has erected a multitude of New Offices, and sent hither swarms of Officers to harrass our people, and eat out their substance.

He has kept among us, in times of peace, Standing Armies without the Consent of our legislatures.

He has affected to render the Military independent of and superior to the Civil power.

He has combined with others to subject us to a jurisdiction foreign to our constitution, and unacknowledged by our laws; giving his Assent to their Acts of pretended Legislation:

For Quartering large bodies of armed troops among us:

For protecting them, by a mock Trial, from punishment for any Murders which they should commit on the Inhabitants of these States:

For cutting off our Trade with all parts of the world:

For imposing Taxes on us without our Consent:

For depriving us in many cases, of the benefits of Trial by jury:

For transporting us beyond Seas to be tried for pretended offences

For abolishing the free System of English Laws in a neighbouring Province, establishing therein an Arbitrary government, and enlarging its Boundaries so as to render it at once an example and fit instrument for introducing the same absolute rule into these Colonies:

For taking away our Charters, abolishing our most valuable Laws, and altering fundamentally the Forms of our Governments:

For suspending our own Legislatures, and declaring themselves invested with power to legislate for us in all cases whatsoever.

He has abdicated Government here, by declaring us out of his Protection and waging War against us.

He has plundered our seas, ravaged our Coasts, burnt our towns, and destroyed the lives of our people.

He is at this time transporting large Armies of foreign Mercenaries to compleat the works of death, desolation and tyranny, already begun with circumstances of Cruelty & perfidy scarcely paralleled in the most barbarous ages, and totally unworthy the Head of a civilized nation.

He has constrained our fellow Citizens taken Captive on the high Seas to bear Arms against their Country, to become the executioners of their friends and Brethren, or to fall themselves by their Hands.

He has excited domestic insurrections amongst us, and has endeavoured to bring on the inhabitants of our frontiers, the merciless Indian Savages, whose known rule of warfare, is an undistinguished destruction of all ages, sexes and conditions.

In every stage of these Oppressions We have Petitioned for Redress in the most humble terms: Our repeated Petitions have been answered only by repeated injury. A Prince whose character is thus marked by every act which may define a Tyrant, is unfit to be the ruler of a free people.

Nor have We been wanting in attentions to our British brethren. We have warned them from time to time of attempts by their legislature to extend an unwarrantable jurisdiction over us. We have reminded them of the circumstances of our emigration and settlement here. We have appealed to their native justice and magnanimity, and we have conjured them by the ties of our common kindred to disavow these usurpations, which, would inevitably interrupt our connections and correspondence. They too have been deaf to the voice of justice and of consanguinity. We must, therefore, acquiesce in the necessity, which denounces our Separation, and hold them, as we hold the rest of mankind, Enemies in War, in Peace Friends.

We, therefore, the Representatives of the united States of America, in General Congress, Assembled, appealing to the Supreme Judge of the world for the rectitude of our intentions, do, in the Name, and by Authority of the good People of these Colonies, solemnly publish and declare, That these United Colonies are, and of Right ought to be Free and Independent States; that they are Absolved from all Allegiance to the British Crown, and that all political connection between them and the State of Great Britain, is and ought to be totally dissolved; and that as Free and Independent States, they have full Power to levy War, conclude Peace, contract Alliances, establish Commerce, and to do all other Acts and Things which Independent States may of right do. — And for the support of this Declaration, with a firm reliance on the protection of divine Providence, we mutually pledge to each other our Lives, our Fortunes and our sacred Honor.

John Hancock

Button Gwinnett
Lyman Hall
Geo Walton.

Wm Hooper
Joseph Hewes,
John Penn

Edward Rutledge.

Thos Heyward Junr.
Thomas Lynch Junr.
Arthur Middleton

Samuel Chase
Wm Paca
Thos Stone
Charles Carroll of Carrollton

George Wythe
Richard Henry Lee
Th Jefferson
Benja Harrison
Thos Nelson jr.
Francis Lightfoot Lee
Carter Braxton

Robt Morris
Benjamin Rush
Benja Franklin
John Morton
Geo Clymer
Jas. Smith.
Geo. Taylor
James Wilson
Geo. Ross
Caesar Rodney
Geo Read
Tho M:Kean

Wm Floyd
Phil. Livingston
Frans. Lewis
Lewis Morris
Richd Stockton
Jno Witherspoon
Fras. Hopkinson
John Hart
Abra Clark

Josiah Bartlett
Wm Whipple
Saml Adams
John Adams
Robt Treat Paine
Elbridge Gerry
Step Hopkins
William Ellery
Roger Sherman
Sam'el Huntington
Wm Williams
Oliver Wolcott
Matthew Thornton

Painting shows Betsy Ross sewing the first American flag while George Washington watches.

The Declaration called the former colonies "Free and Independent States." The Congressmen pledged to support the Declaration with their "Lives...Fortunes and...sacred Honor."

THE DECLARATION'S EFFECT

The Declaration *said* that the colonies were free. But to make those words come true, George Washington's army had to win the Revolutionary War against England.

The Declaration helped the United States win that war. Americans were more willing to fight now that they had their own country. Other nations, especially France, were more willing to side with the United States now that it had declared its independence. The Americans won the Revolutionary War in 1781.

Americans have been proud of the Declaration of Independence for over two hundred years. The Declaration reminds us of why America broke away from England long ago. It also reminds us that it is

wrong to be prejudiced
against people due to their
color or religion, because all
people "are created equal."
It inspires us to help build
a world where everyone
will be born with the rights
to "Life, Liberty and the
pursuit of Happiness."

WORDS YOU SHOULD KNOW

Boston Tea Party(BAW • stun TEE PAR • tee)—the 1773 raid in which Americans destroyed a large tea shipment to protest the tax on tea

century(SENCH • ree)—one hundred years

colony(KAHL • uh • nee)—a settlement outside a parent country and ruled by the parent country

committee(kuh • MIH • tee)—a group of persons named to do a special job

continent(KAHN • tih • nent)—one of Earth's largest landmasses

Continental Congress(kahn • tih • NEN • til KAHNG • ress)—the body of lawmakers that governed the country before the United States Congress was formed

Declaration of Independence(dek • la • RAY • shun UV in • dih • PEN • dints)—the paper stating that the Thirteen American Colonies had become the United States of America

delegate(DEL • ih • git)—a person who acts for other people

Fourth of July—the American holiday celebrating the adoption of the Declaration of Independence; also called Independence Day

Hessians(HESH • inz)—German soldiers who fought for the English during the Revolutionary War

independence(in • dih • PEN • dints)—the quality of standing on one's own

liberty(LIH • ber • tee)—freedom

Loyalists(LOY • ul • ists)—Americans who remained loyal to the English during the Revolutionary War

majority(ma • JORE • ih • tee)—more than half of a number

permanent(PER • mih • nent)—lasting

prejudice(PREH • juh • diss) — a dislike of people due to such qualities as their color, religion, or sex

"redcoats"(RED • kotes) — the Americans' nickname for the English soldiers (due to the color of their uniforms)

Revolutionary War(reh • vih • LOO • shun • air • ee WAR) — the war the United States fought to become free of England; also called the American Revolution

slavery(SLAY • ver • ee) — a practice in which people are owned by other people

states(STAITS) — what the colonies called themselves upon declaring their independence

taxes(TAX • is) — money people pay to support government

Thomas Jefferson(TOM • is JEFF • er • sun — the author of the Declaration of Independence and later a United States President

unanimous(yoo • NAN • ih • mus) — having the vote or support of all

INDEX

About the Author

Dennis Fradin attended Northwestern University on a partial creative writing scholarship and was graduated in 1967. His previous books include the Young People's Stories of Our States series for Childrens Press, and Bad Luck Tony *for Prentice-Hall. In the True Book series Dennis has written about astronomy, farming, comets, archaeology, movies, the space lab, explorers, and pioneers. He is married and the father of three children.*